Good Old Tunes

HARP & LYRE

LULLABIES

Easy and Beautiful Harmonies
for 15 strings tuned to key of C

arranged by Susan Call Hutchison

Simple and sweet as the memory of being rocked to sleep.

Complete with sing-along lyrics, these gentle, soothing lullabies are perfect for home practice and playing, and also a charming addition to group classes, recitals, music therapy, and hospice ministry.

Whether you are a beginner with a new lyre or a seasoned harpist who loves to improvise over chords, this enchanting collection will quickly become a favorite.

All songs are playable on a 15-string unlevered harp or lyre, tuned to the key of C, from middle C to the C two octaves above. Songs include chords, so you can improvise even more intricate harmonies using lyre or any type of harp. Or work up a dreamy lullaby duet with a teacher or friend on harp, piano, guitar, or any other harmonizing instrument or voice.

Contents

Introduction: Lyre and Harp Lullabies

This was a fun book to put together!

It's such a natural combination, lullabies and harps. Imagine how many generations in different cultures have used the dreamy, relaxing sounds of the lyre or harp to calm a child or comfort someone to sleep.

My own background is Anglo-American, so the lullabies in my memories are based on Mother Goose nursery rhymes, with tunes and harmonies that fall easily under the fingers on an un-levered harp. Most of the tunes will be familiar to anyone of the same background. I confess I wrote a few of the nursery rhyme melodies myself, but since my own babies are in their 30s and 40s now, I don't have a problem sneaking my work into a volume called Good Old Tunes.

A couple of German lullabies worked well, too, with the concept of a 15 string (2 octave) unlevered harp. I found two lullabies by Johannes Brahms. He wrote not only his famous "Cradle Song," but also popularized a traditional lullaby, *"Sandmännchen."* I loosely translated the German lyrics to include in this book.

I found an American gospel song and some folk lullabies to tuck into the collection, too.

Lyrics are important to me, not only because I imagine these songs being played and sung by parents to children, but because the words of songs are so important in guiding choices in musical phrasing, dynamics, and even harmony.

Don't let the simplicity of these songs fool you. They are full of opportunities for self-expression and musicality. That's one reason I also envision these tunes as the basis for improvised harmonies and perhaps student-teacher duets, recital or school performances or senior center activities.

I do hope that those of you involved in music therapy and hospice ministries will find these gentle, nostalgic tunes a helpful addition to your repertoire. They were written especially for harps that are easiest to travel with and play at a bedside.

Susan Call Hutchison
Musical Director
Good Old Tunes Publications

Contact me at sus@goodoldtunes.com

Good Old Tunes

Sleep, Baby, Sleep

Traditional Lullaby Lyrics

Susan Call Hutchison

All the Pretty Little Horses

Traditional
arranged by Susan Call Hutchison

Adagio

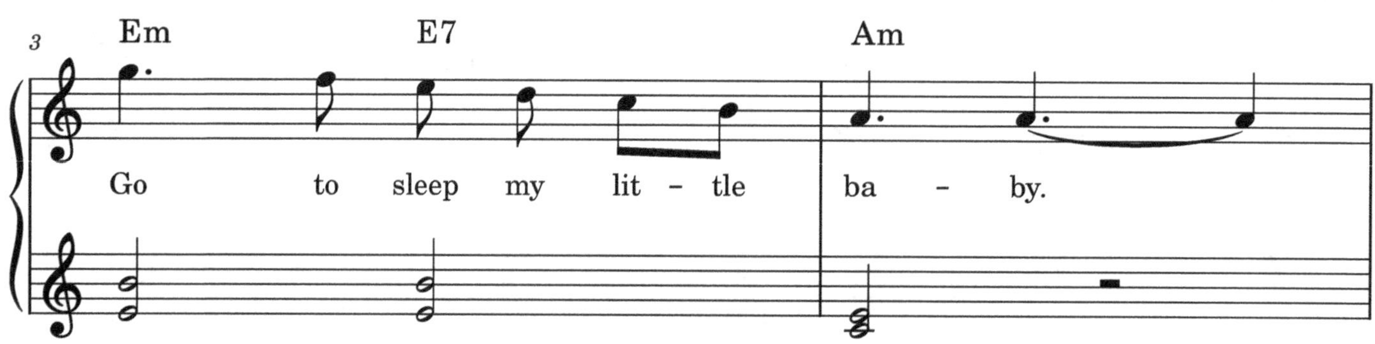

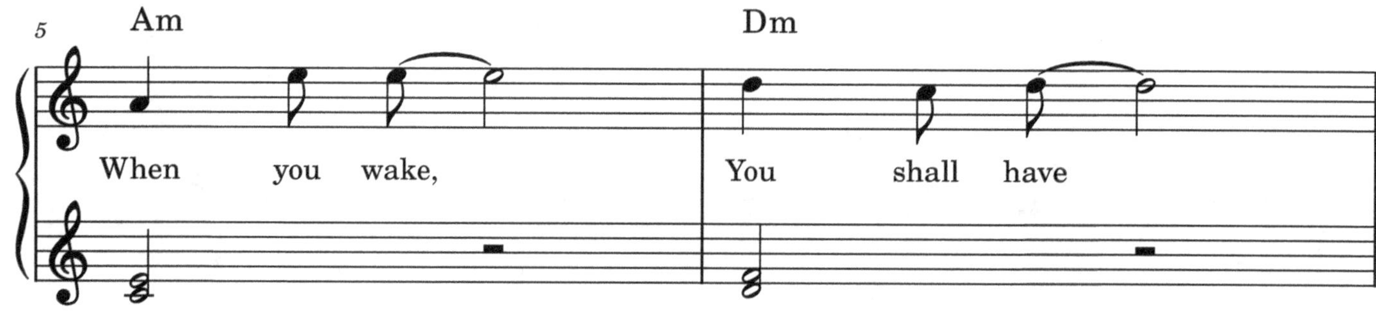

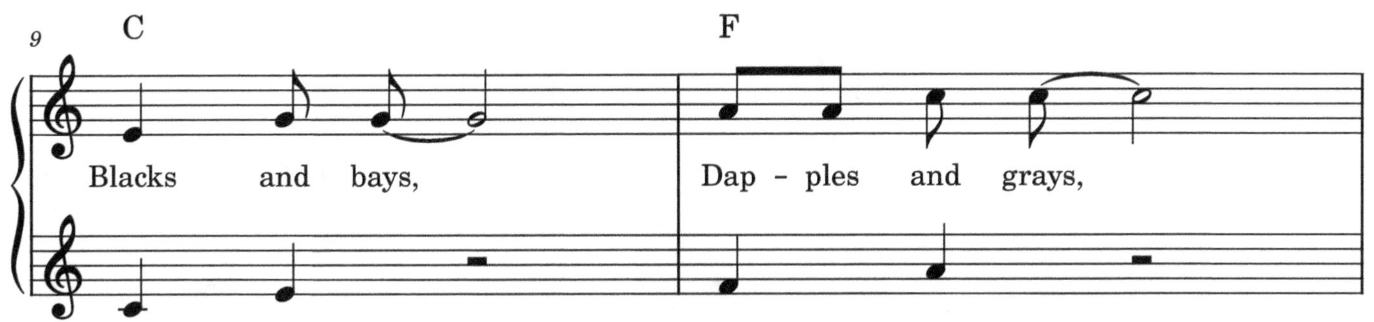
9
C
F
Blacks and bays,
Dap - ples and grays,

11
Em
E7
Am
Coach and six - a - lit - tle hors - es.

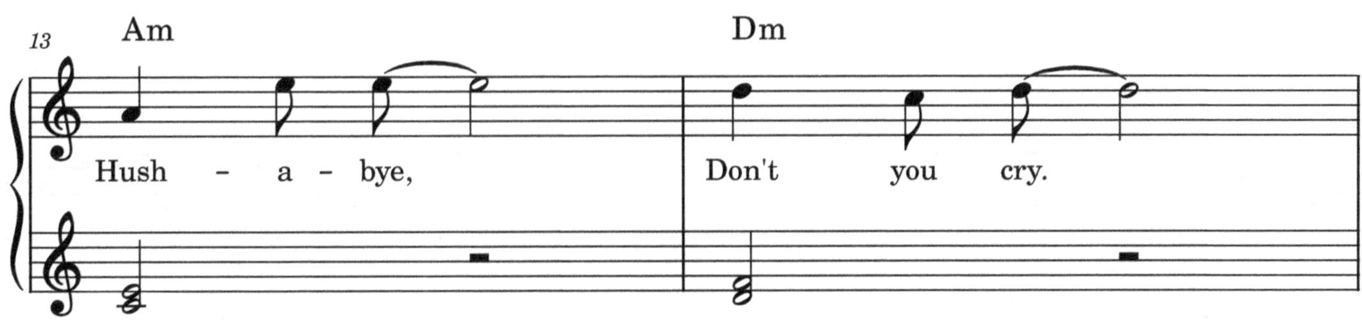
13
Am
Dm
Hush - a - bye,
Don't you cry.

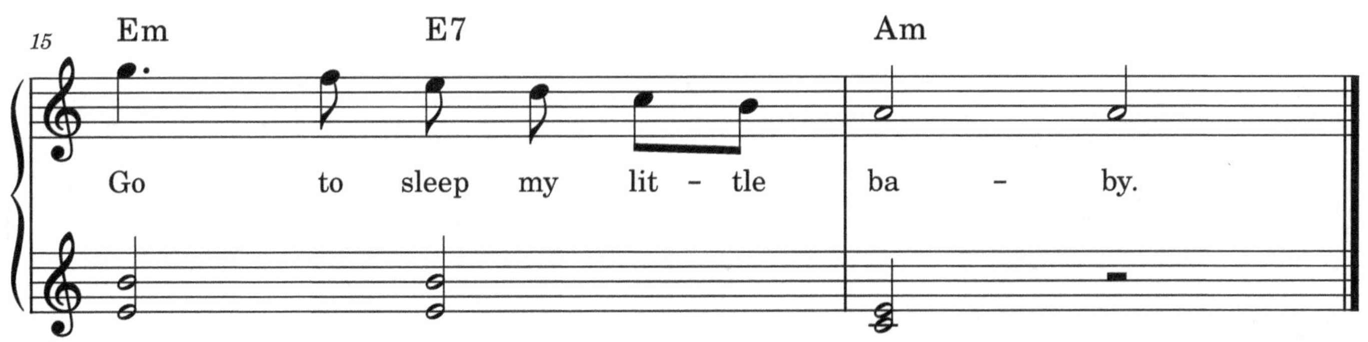
15
Em
E7
Am
Go to sleep my lit - tle ba - by.

Good Old Tunes
Hush, Little Baby

Traditional
arranged by Susan Call Hutchison

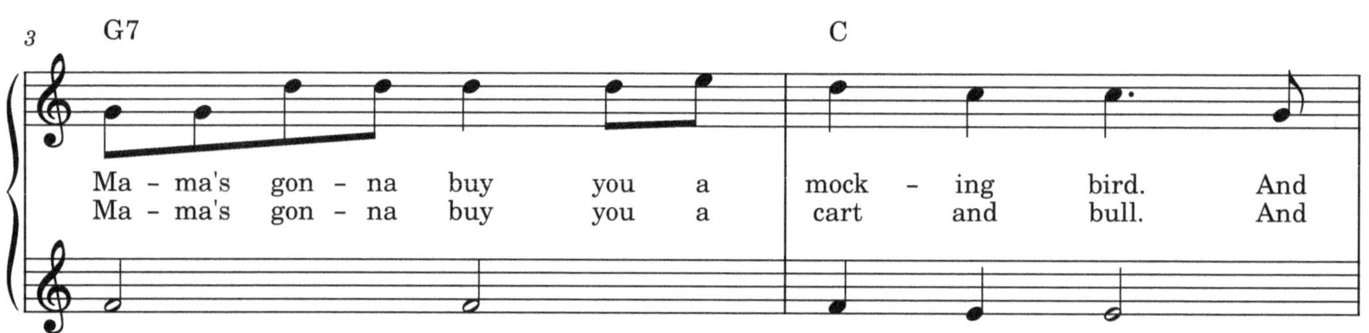

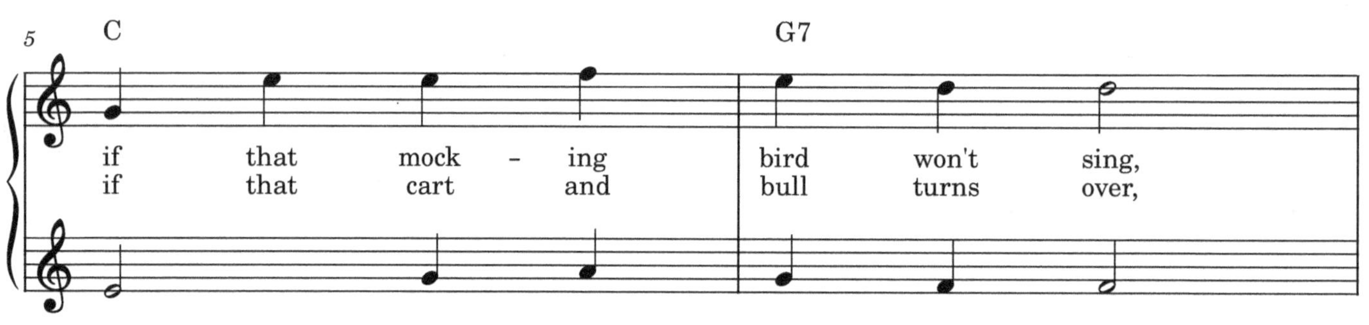

C
G7
if that dia - mond ring turns brass.
if that dog named Rover won't bark,
G7
C
Ma - ma's gon - na buy you a look - ing glass. And
Ma - ma's gon - na buy you a horse and cart. And
C
G7
if that look - ing glass gets broke,
if that horse and cart fall down, You'll
1. G7
C
Ma - ma's gon - na buy you a bil - ly goat And
2. G7
C
still be the sweet - est lit - tle ba - by in town.

Good Old Tunes

Bye, Baby Bunting

Traditional
arranged by Susan Call Hutchison

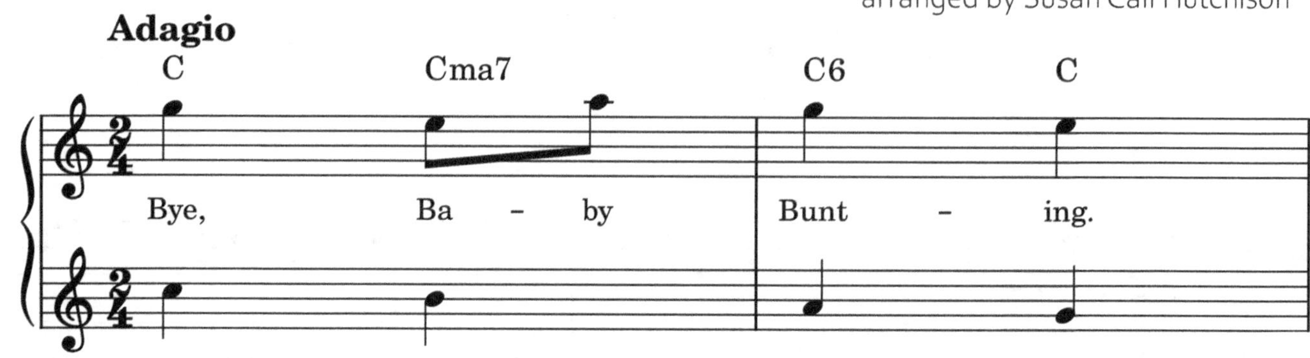

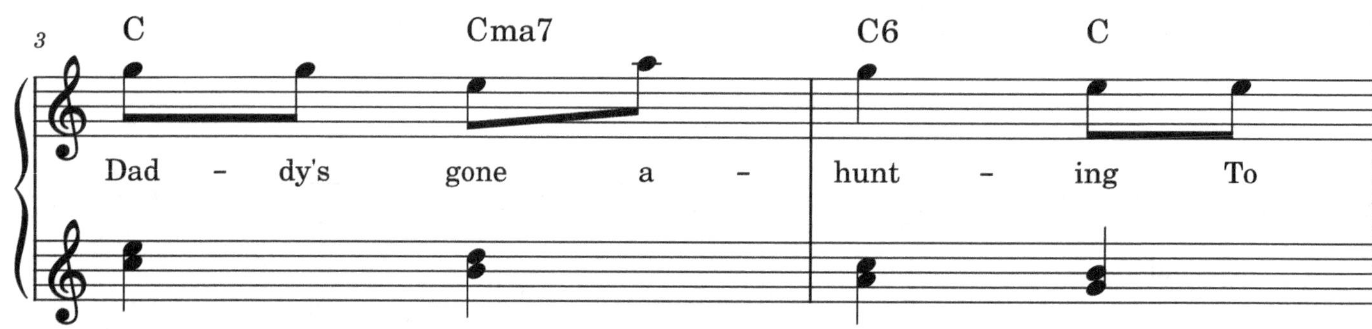

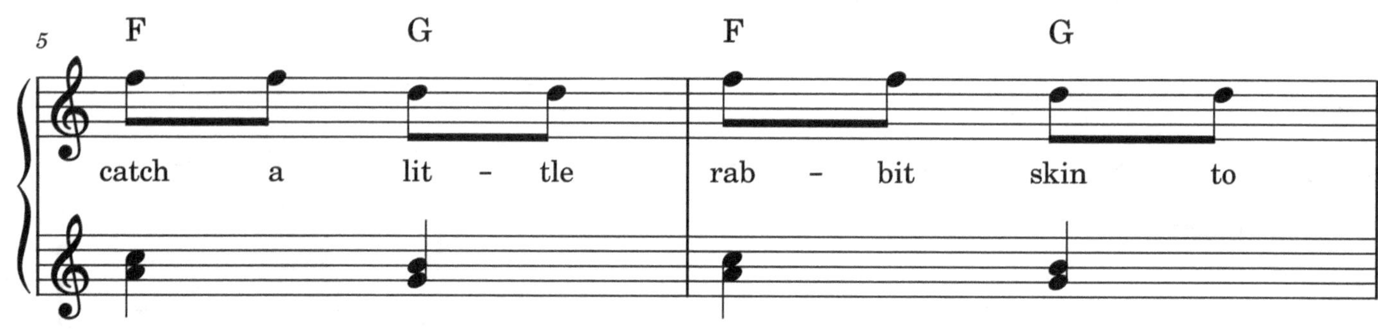

Row, Row, Row Your Boat

Traditional
arranged by Susan Call Hutchison

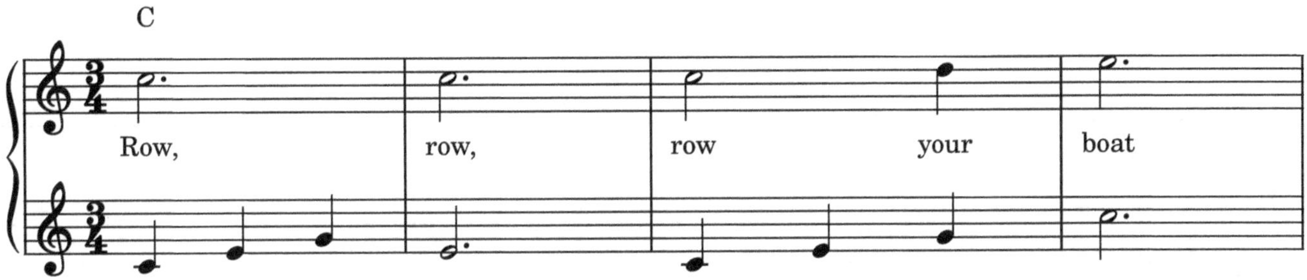

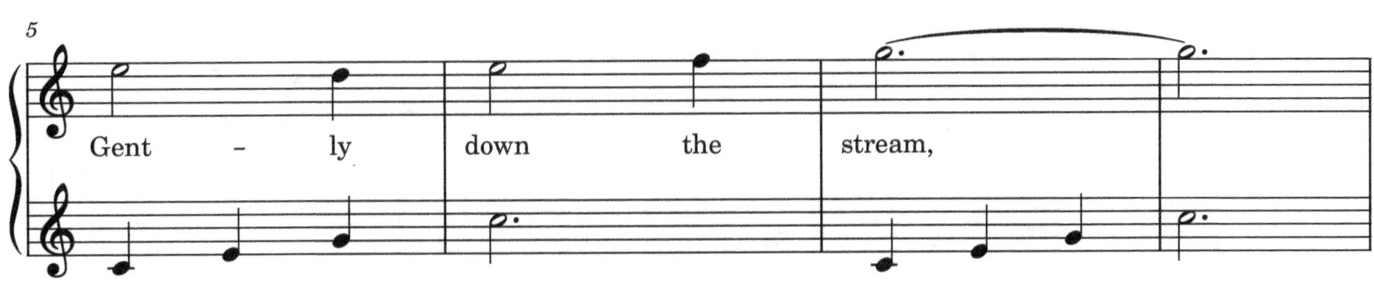

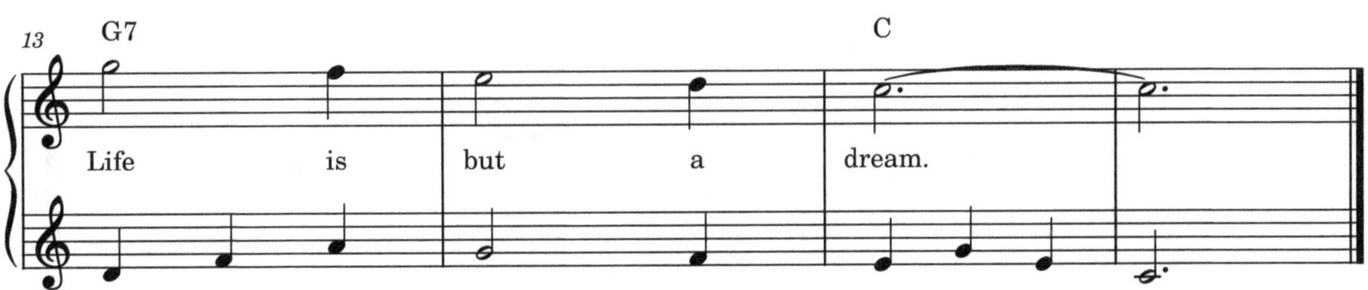

Good Old Tunes
Star Light, Star Bright

Traditional

Susan Call Hutchison

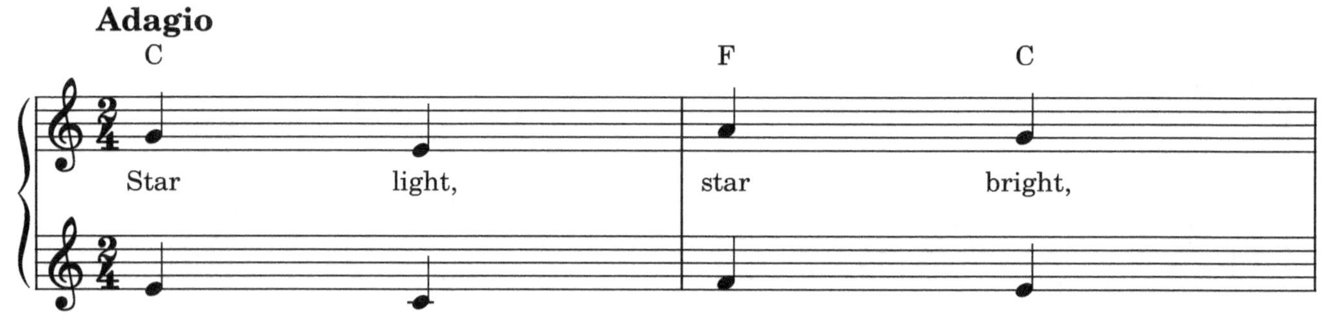

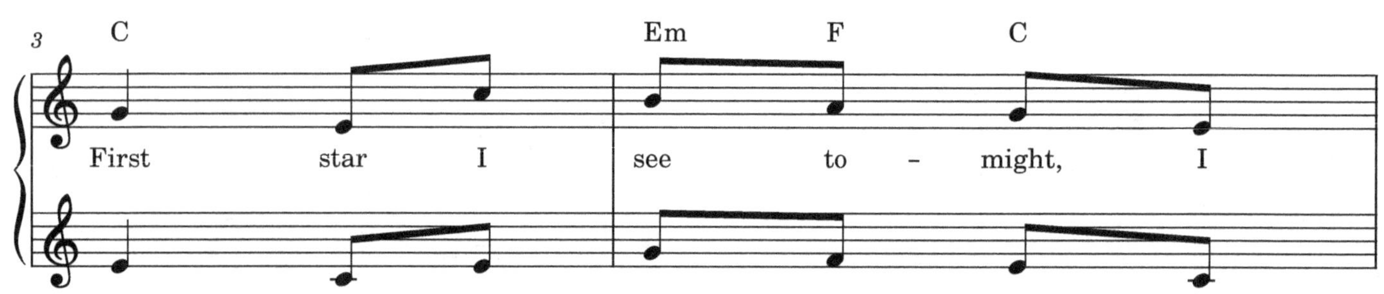

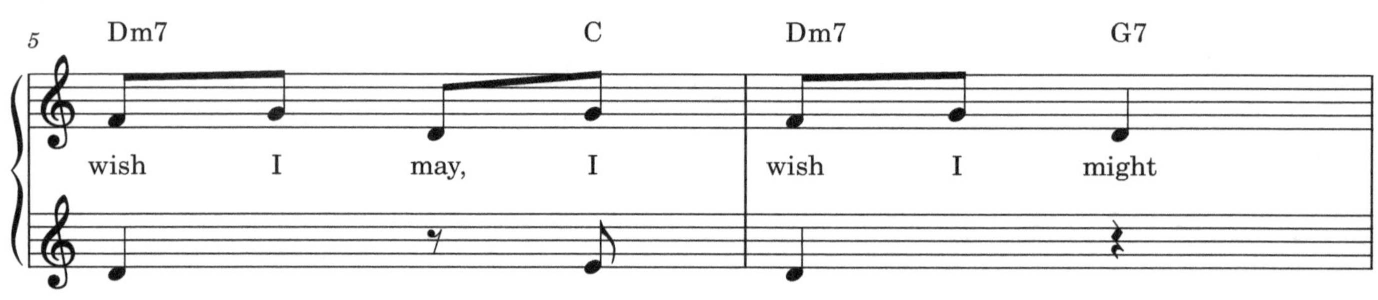

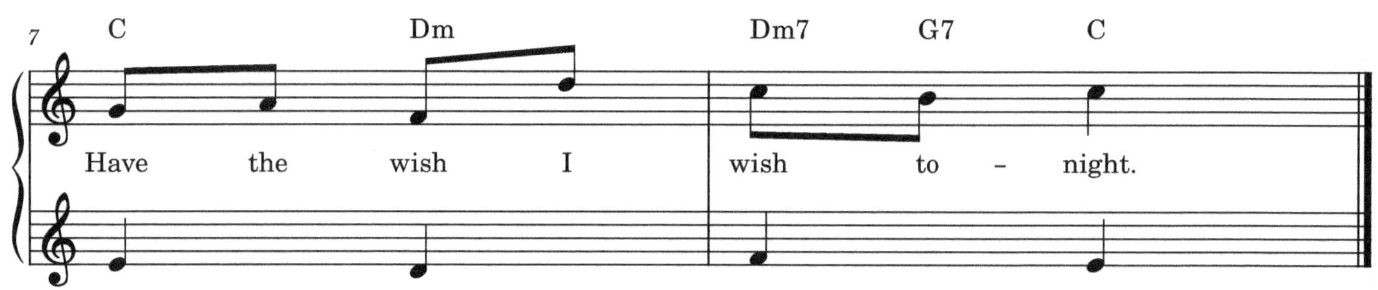

Twinkle, Twinkle, Little Star

Traditional
arranged by Susan Call Hutchison

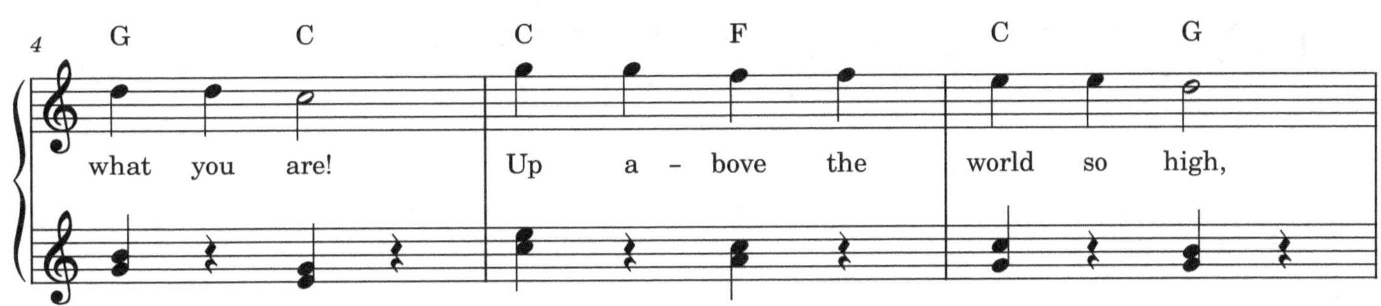

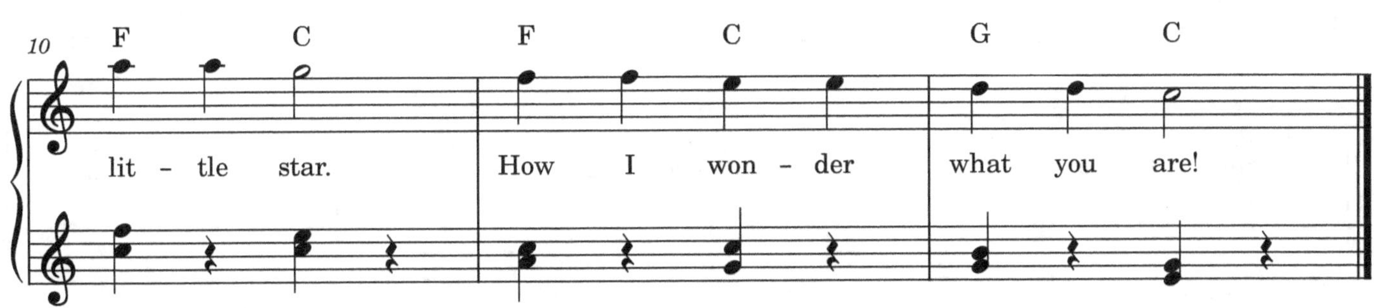

The Little Sandman
(Sandmännchen)

Lyrics by Susan Call Hutchison
based on anonymous 1857 German lyrics

German lullaby adapted by Johannes Brahms
Arranged by Susan Call Hutchison

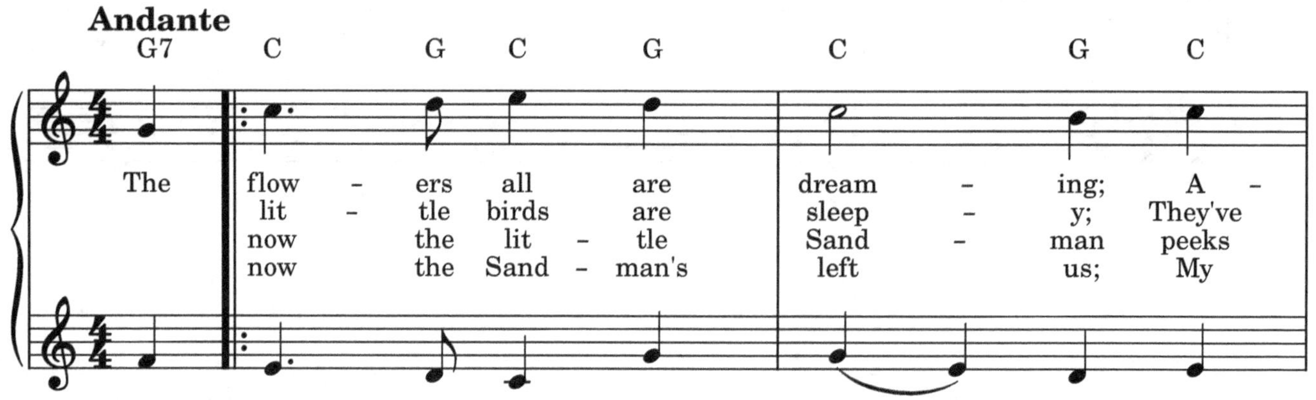

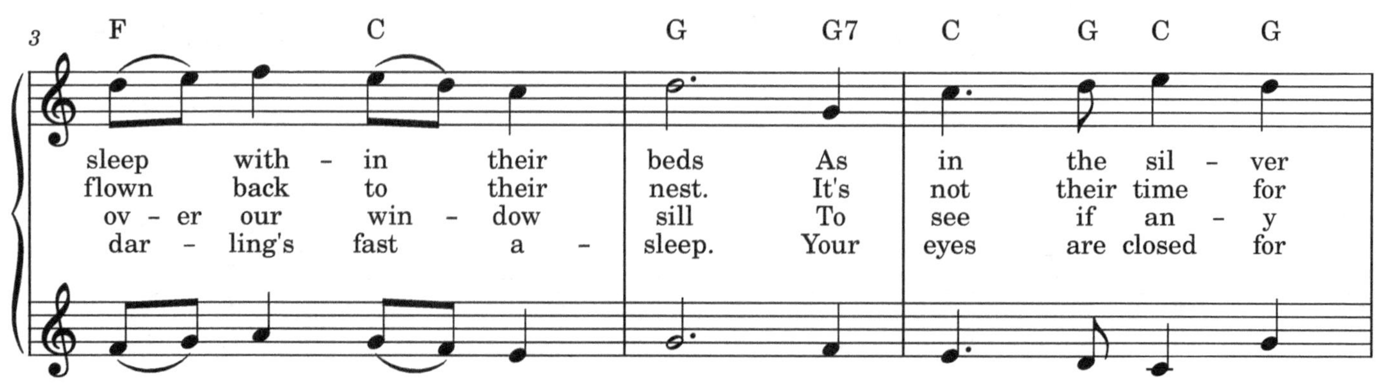

9
C   F   C   F   C   F   G   C
blos - oms   from   the   ap - ple   tree   now
list - en   to   the   crick - ets   who
spreads a   lit - tle   mag - ic   sand;   We
mor - row   you   will   greet   me   with

11
G7   C   G7   C   G7
float   as   in   a   dream.   So   go   to   sleep;
sing   all   through the   night.   So   go   to   sleep;
rub   our   wear - y   eyes   and go   to   sleep.
eyes   so   clear   and   bright.   But un - til then,

14
C   G   C   G   C   F   C   Am   Dm   C   G7
Go   to sleep my lit - tle   dar - ling,   Go   go
Go   to sleep my lit - tle   dar - ling,   Go   to
Go   to sleep my lit - tle   dar - ling,   Go   to
Stay   a - sleep my lit - tle   dar - ling,   Stay a

1. 2. 3.   4.
16
C   G7   C
sleep.   2.The   sleep!
sleep.   3.And
sleep.   4.And

Good Old Tunes
All Through the Night

Sir Harold Boulton

Welsh Air
arranged by Susan Call Hutchison

Dm   C   Dm   C   F   C   Dm   C
Soft   the   drow - sy   hours   are   creep - ing,
F   C   Dm   C   C   G7   Am   G
Hill   and   vale   in   slum - ber   sleep - ing,
C   F   D   G
I   my   lov - ing   vi - gil   keep - ing
F   G   G7   C
All   through   the   night.

Good Old Tunes
Hickory, Dickory, Dock

Traditional
arranged by Susan Call Hutchison

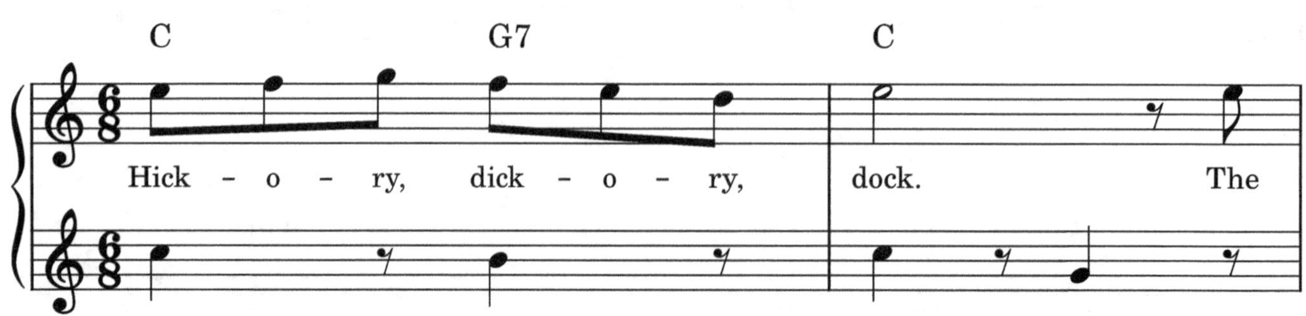

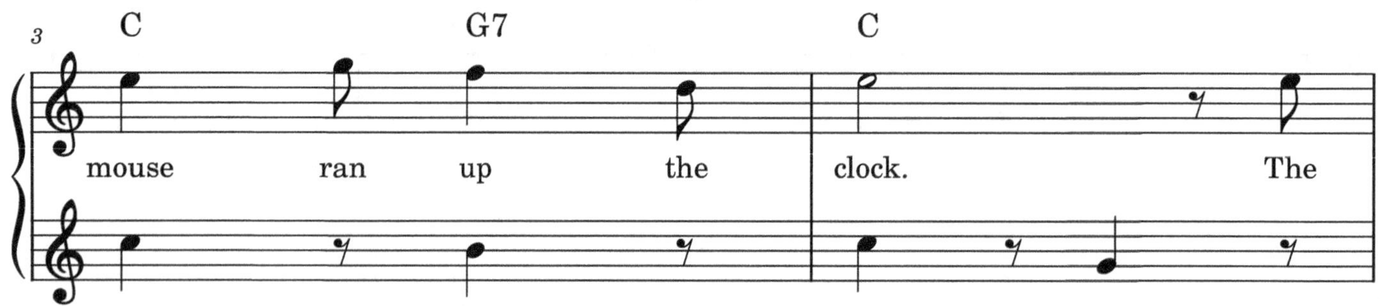

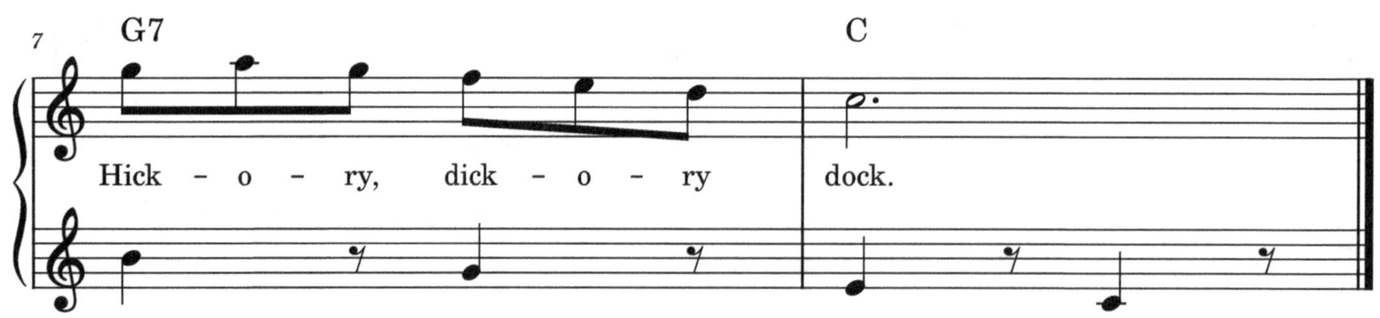

Diddle, Diddle, Dumpling, My Son John

Traditional nursery rhyme
with lyrics added by the composer

Susan Call Hutchison

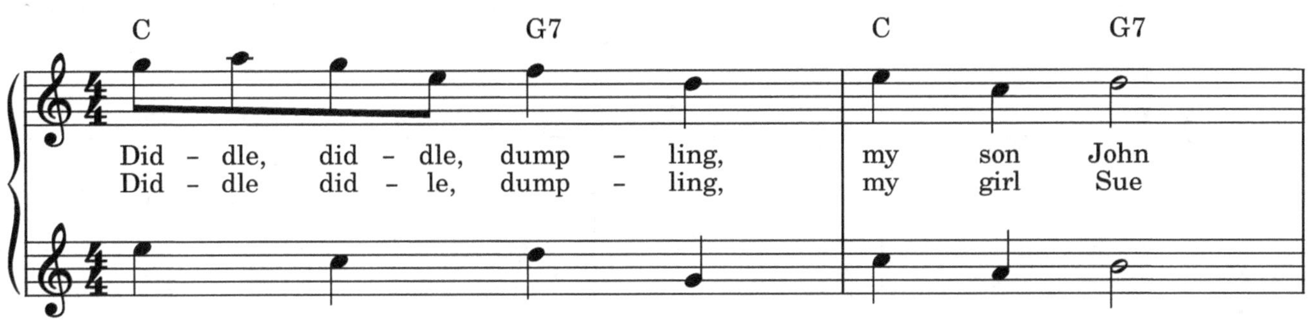

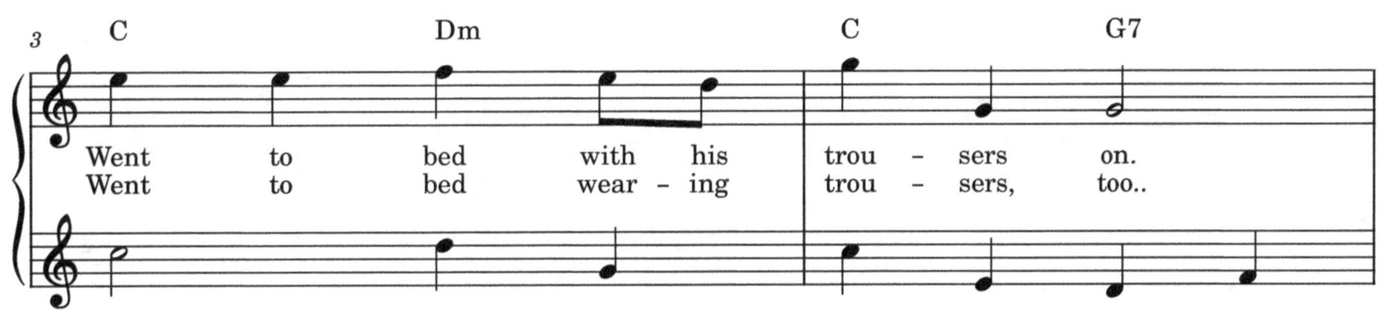

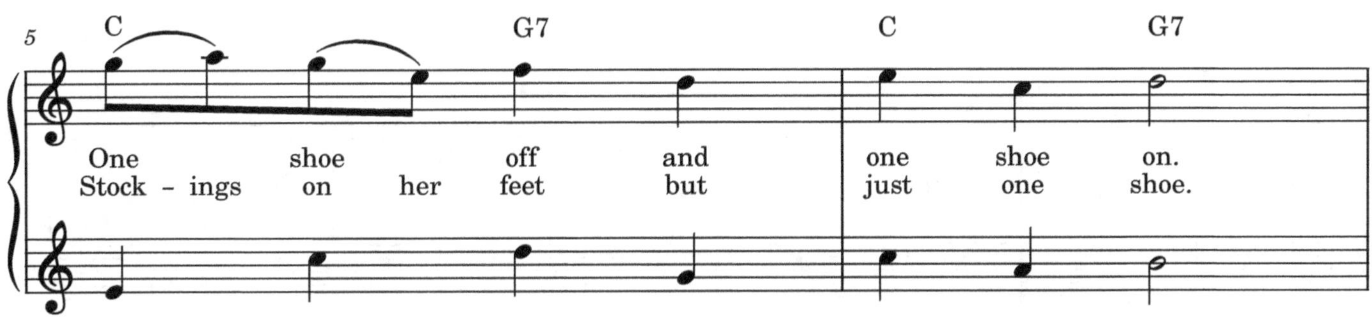

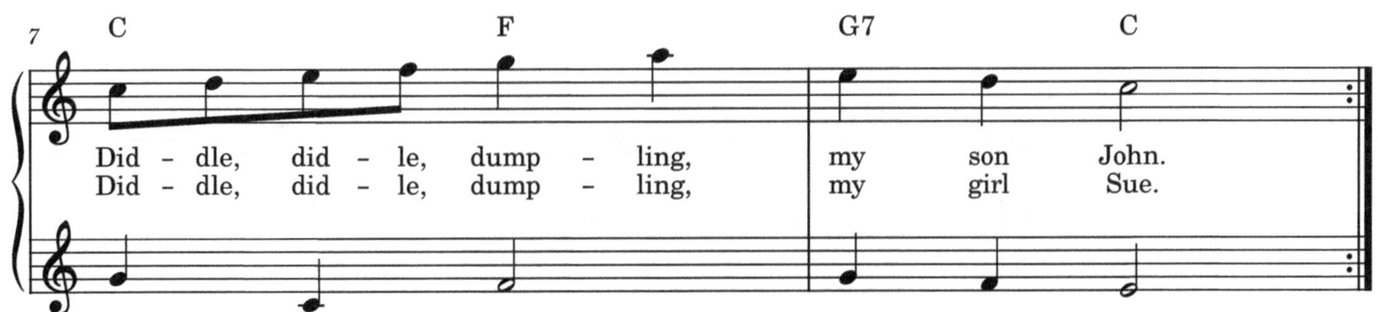

Hey, Diddle, Diddle, the Cat and the Fiddle

Traditional Nursery Rhyme

Susan Call Hutchison

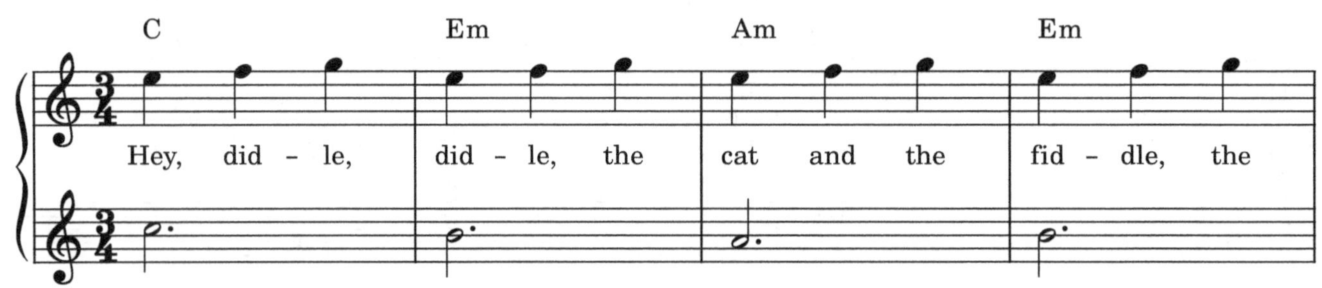

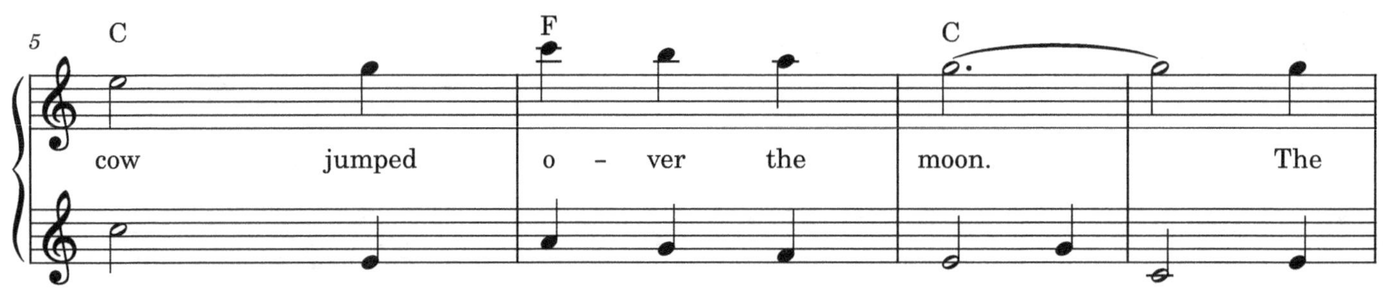

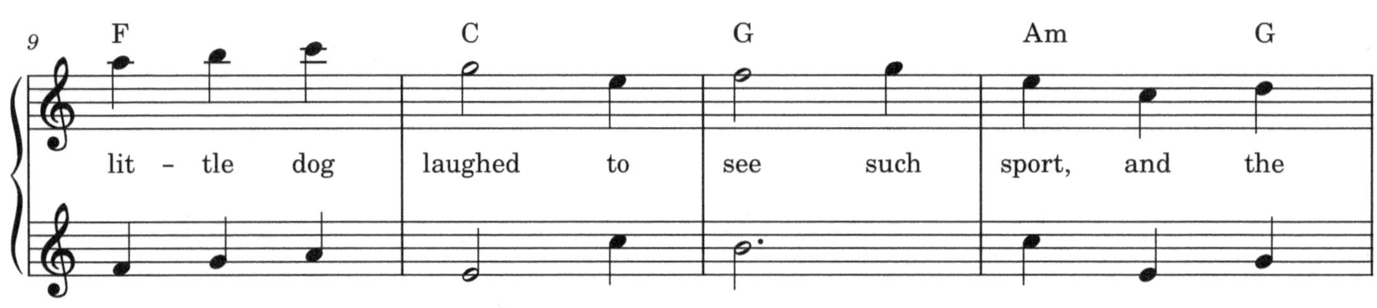

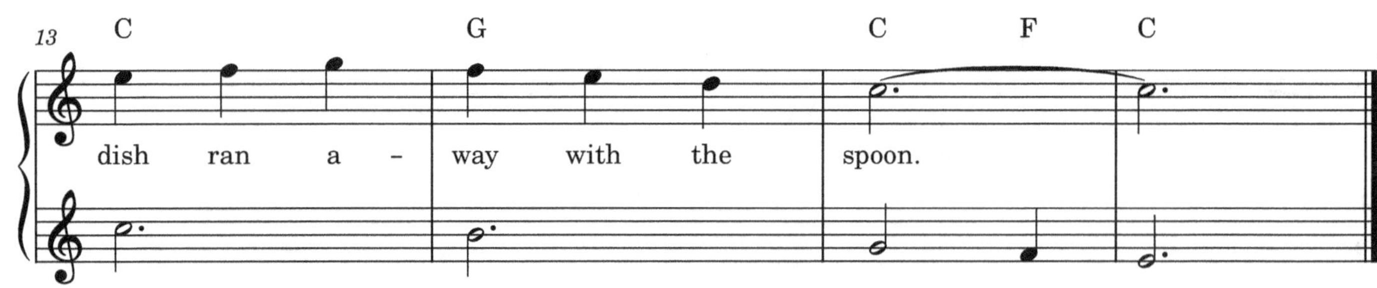

Good Old Tunes

Baa, Baa, Black Sheep

Traditional
arranged by Susan Call Hutchison

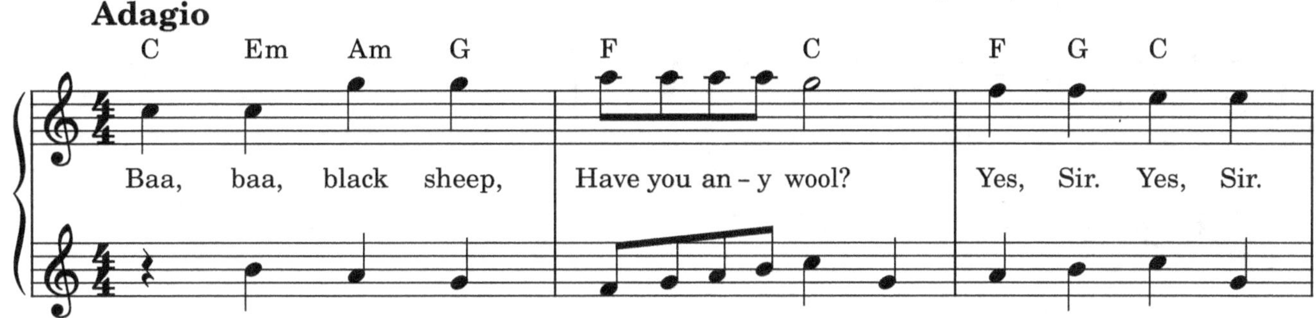

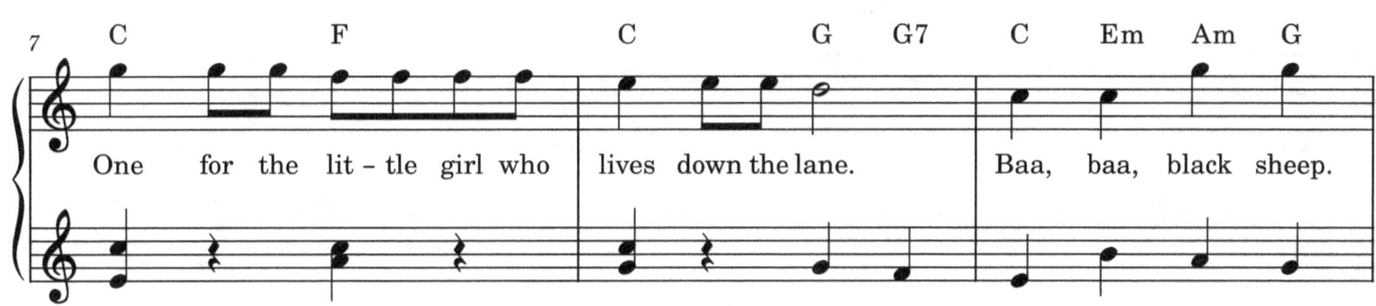

Good Old Tunes

Little Bo Peep

Traditional Nursery Rhyme

Susan Call Hutchison

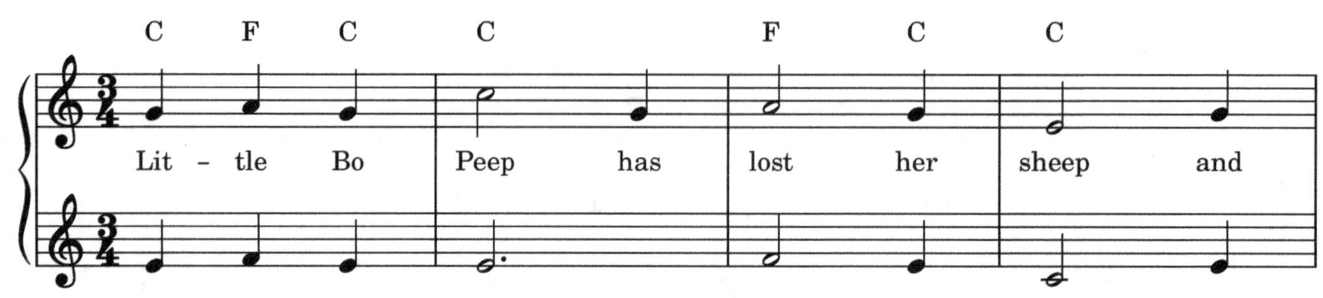

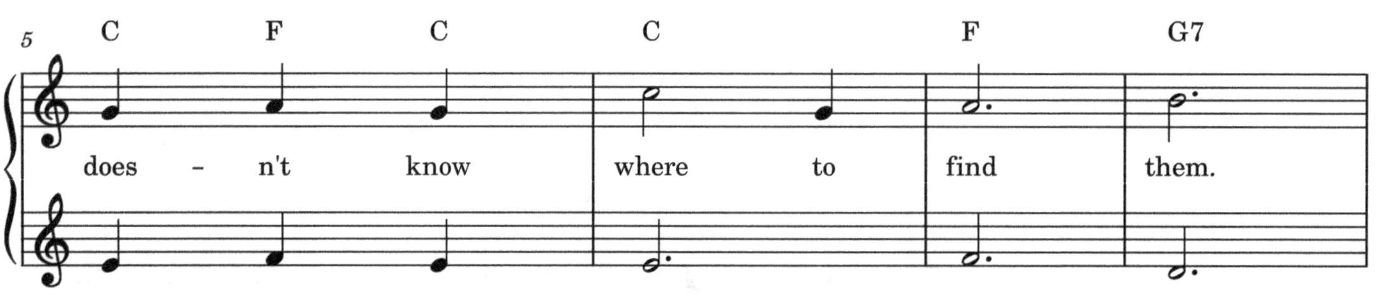

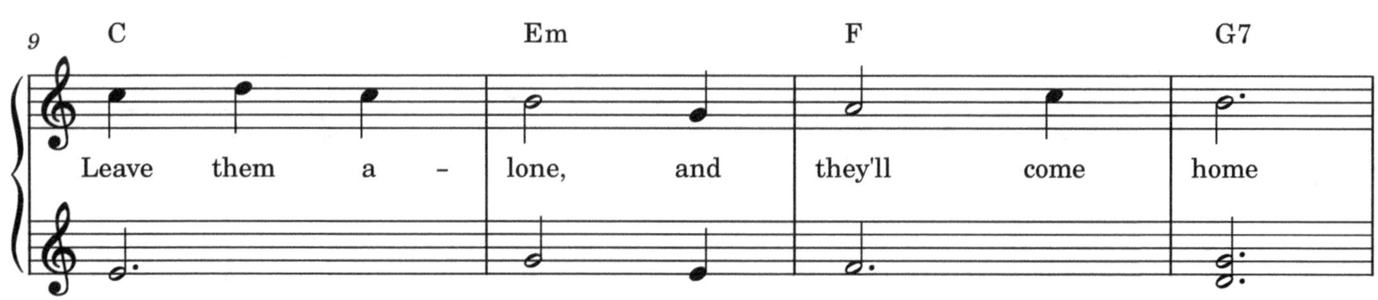

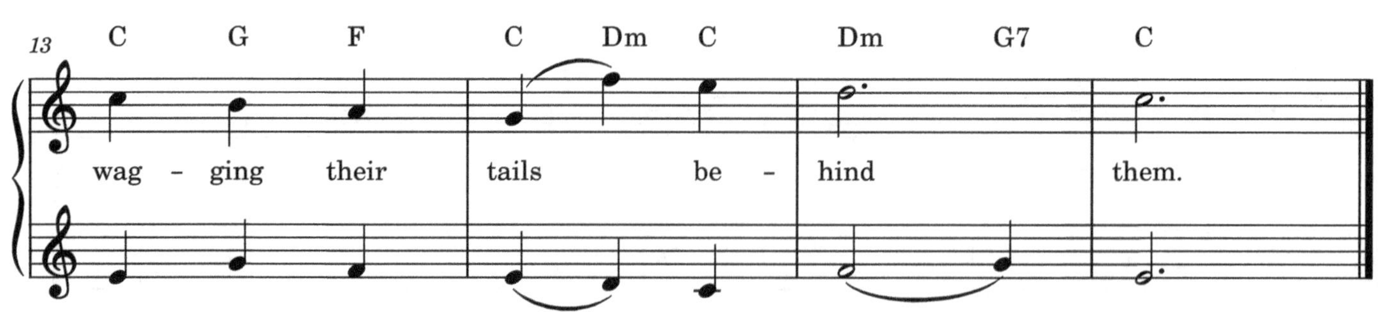

Good Old Tunes

Little Boy Blue, Come Blow Your Horn

Traditional Nursery Rhyme

Susan Call Hutchison

Good Old Tunes

Oranges and Lemons

Traditional English Nursery Rhyme
Arranged by Susan Call Hutchison

This piece may be played an octave higher on a 15 string harp or lyre tuned in C from middle C to the C two ocataves above.

Andante

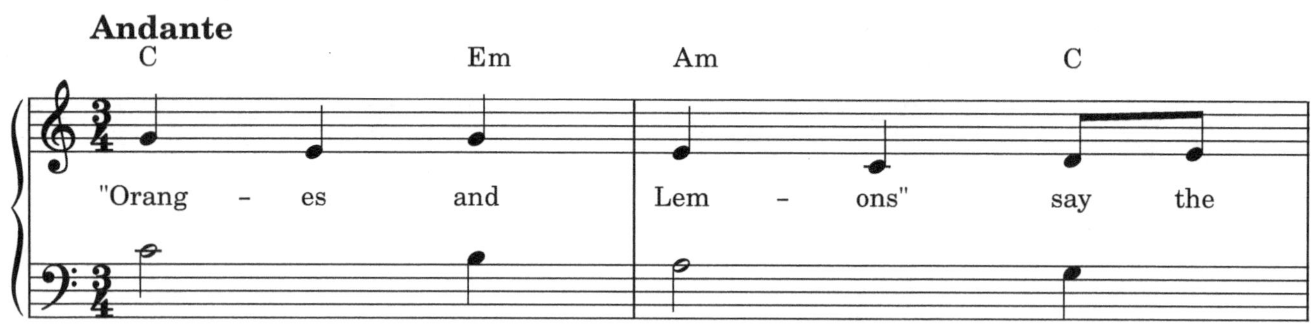

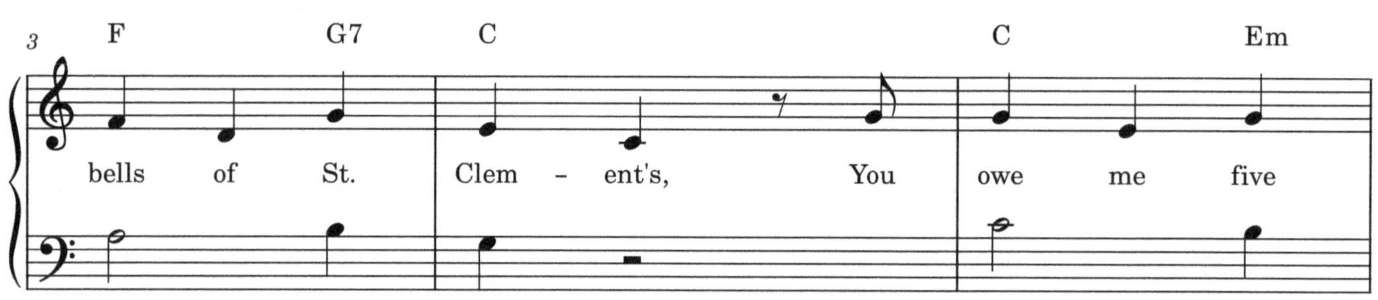

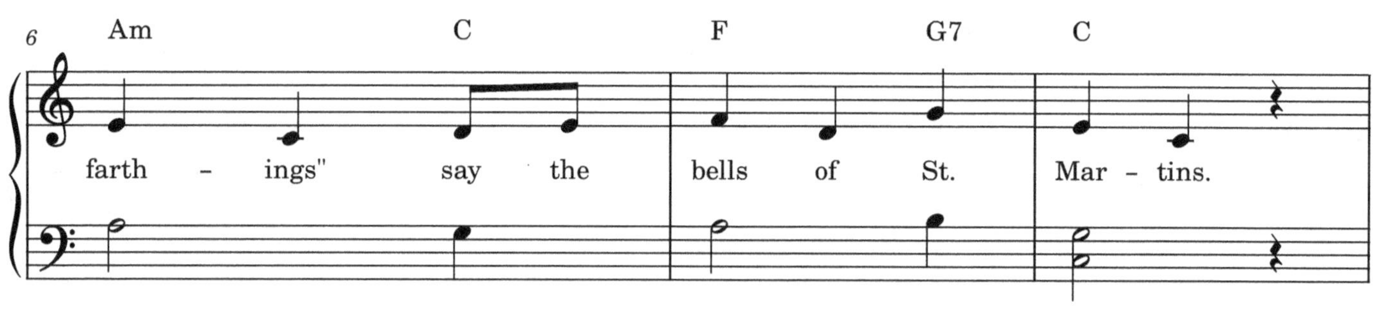

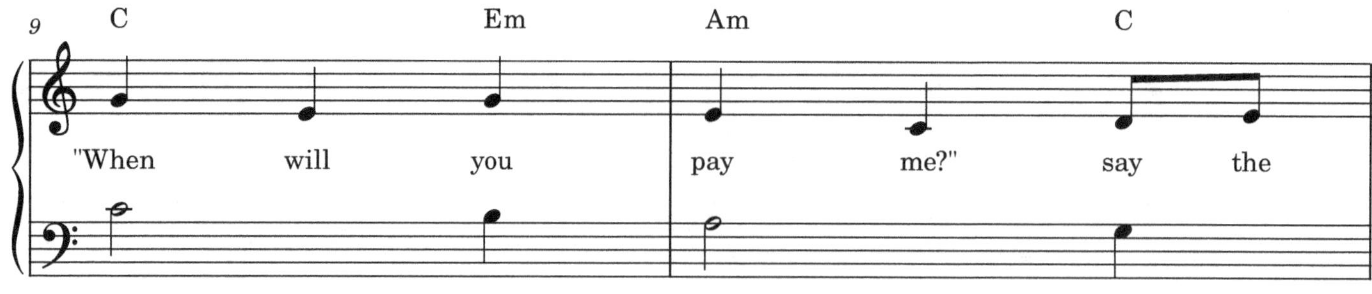

F   G7   C   C   Em
bells   of   Old   Bail - ey.   "When   I   get
Am   C   F   G7   C
rich,"   say   the   bell   of   Shore - ditch.
"When   will   that   be?"   say   the   bells   of   Step -
C
ney.   "Im   sure   I   don't   know!"   says   the
slowing
Am
slowe and stately
F   G7   C
great   bell   of   Bow.

Good Old Tunes

All Night, All Day

(Angels Watching Over Me)

Traditional Spritual
arranged by Susan Call Hutchison

Andante

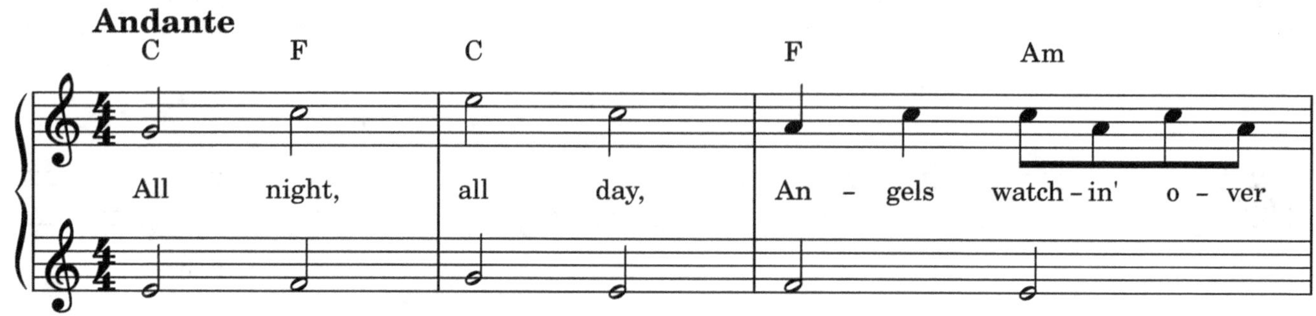

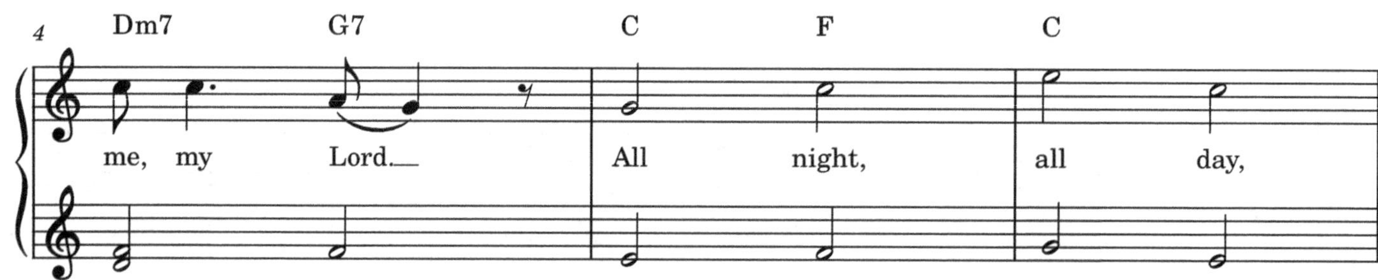

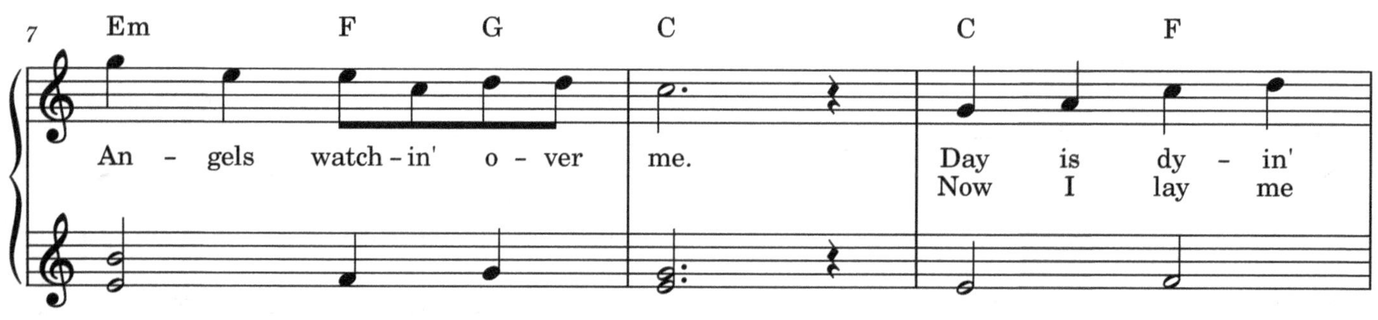

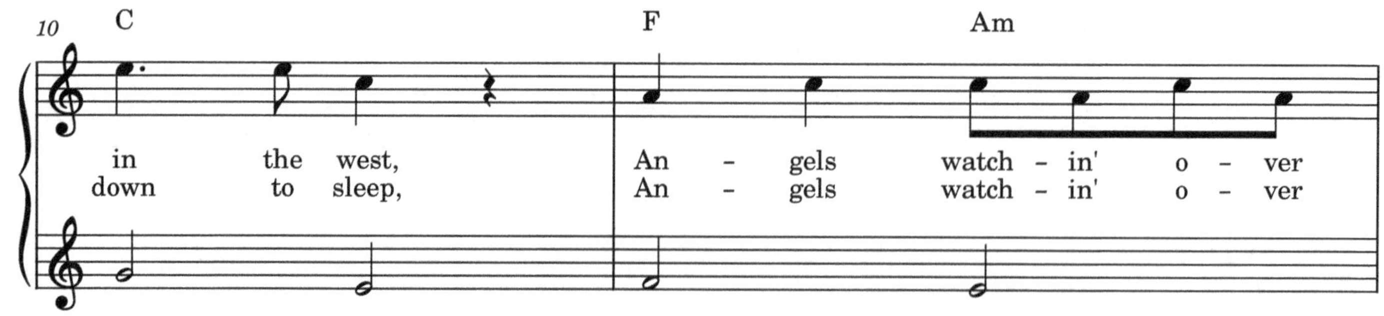

12
F   G7   C   F
me, my   Lord.___   Sleep   my   child   and
me, my   Lord.___   Pray   the   Lord   my
14
E7sus   E7   Am   Em   F   G7   C
take   your rest,   An - gels   watch - in'   o - ver   me.
soul   to keep,   An - gels   watch - in'   o - ver   me.
17
C   F   C   F   Am
All   night,   all   day,   An - gels   watch - in'   o - ver
20
Dm7   G7   C   F   C
me, my   Lord.___   All   night,   all   day,
23
Em   F   G   C
An - gels   watch - in'   o - ver   me.

Good Old Tunes

Cradle Song
(Brahms' Lullaby)

Johannes Brahms
arranged by Susan Call Hutchison

Lyricist unknown

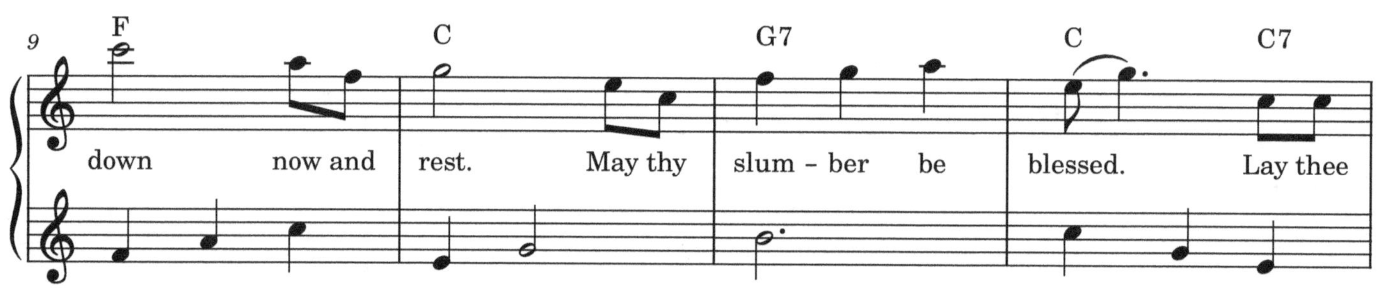

B
C
G
Lul-la - by and good night, Thy moth - er's de - light. Bright

G7
C
C7
an - gels be - side My dar - ling a - bide. They will

F
C
G7
C
C7
guard thee at rest, Thou shalt wake on my breast. They shall

F
C
F
G7
C
guard thee at rest. Thou shalt wake on my breast.

Rock-a-Bye Baby

Traditional Lullaby
arranged by Susan Call Hutchison

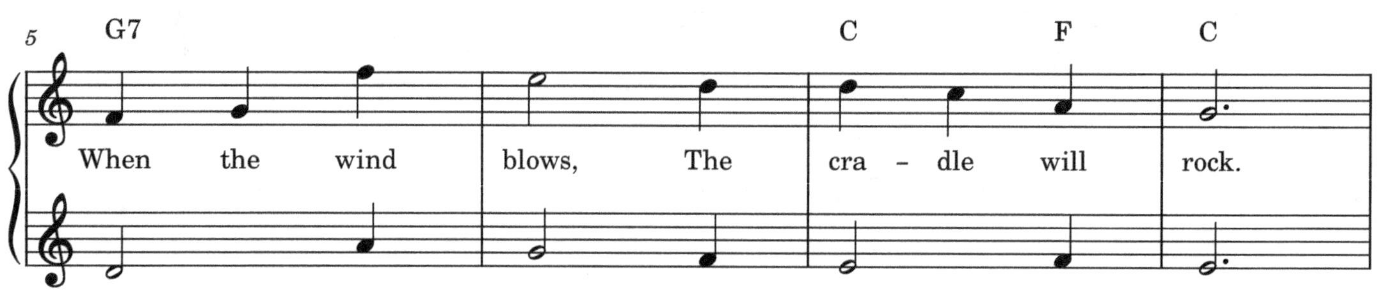

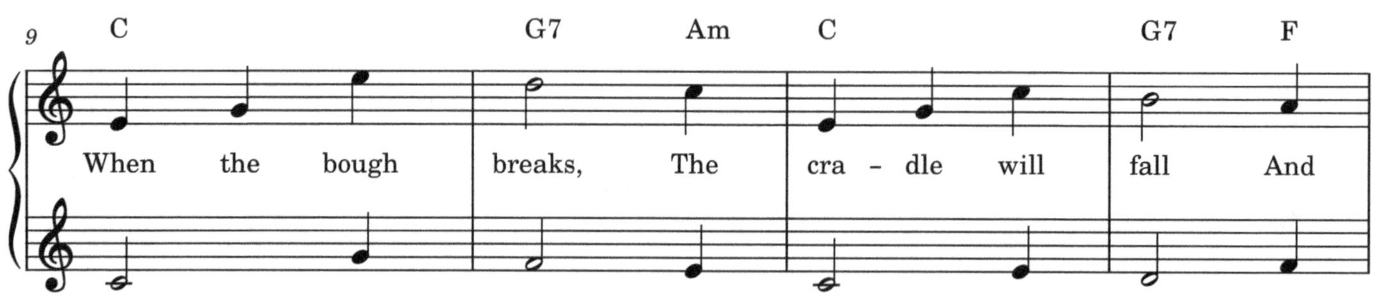

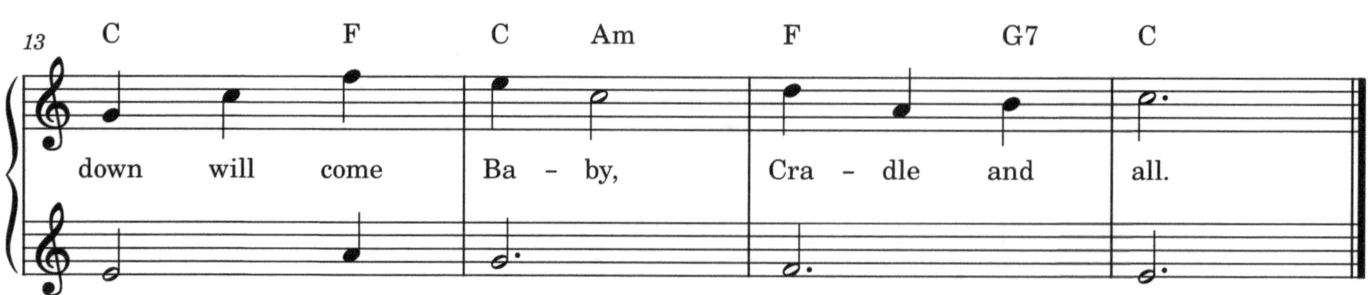